Scrum

Using Agile Planning, Sprint, Advanced Software, and Team Management

By Sally Stephens

Table of Contents

INTRO: WHAT DOES THE SCRUM METHOD ENTAIL? 3

CHAPTER 1: WHAT IS SCRUM? 5

CHAPTER 2: SCRUM MASTERS 7

CHAPTER 3: SCRUM IN THE GLOBAL COMMUNITY 10

CHAPTER 4: LESSENING RISKS THROUGH SCRUM 12

CHAPTER 5: SCRUM AND PITFALLS TO PREVENT INDEFINITELY 14

CHAPTER 6: UNDERSTANDING A SCRUM MASTER, A PRODUCT OWNER, AND DEVELOPMENT TEAM 17

CHAPTER 7: SOME COMMON PROBLEMS THAT A SCRUM MASTER FACES 19

CHAPTER 8: SCRUM-AGILE PROJECT MANAGEMENT SOFTWARE 22

CHAPTER 9: SIX ACTIONS TO A SCRUM CHANGE 24

CHAPTER 10: SCRUM EFFORT ESTIMATES AND STORY POINTS 26

CHAPTER 11: WHAT IS VIRTUAL SCRUM AND HOW IS IT APPLIED? 29

INTRO: WHAT DOES THE SCRUM METHOD ENTAIL?

AGILE SOFTWARE DEVELOPMENT

Agile software development is a popular technique used by various software application designers to prepare and create entirely functioning products for their clients. Each agile methodology skillfully combines both standard and modern ideas in a way that's rapidly understood and adopted by developers. An agile methodology called Scrum is talked about throughout this book. Scrum, better called a framework, is an agile approach to software application development that promotes team work. This means that a team of designers doesn't get a pre-determined guide defining how each step is to be carried out on a project. Decision making is mainly done by the group itself without getting guidelines from a leader or manager.

So the Scrum team is expected to be totally autonomous and organized so as to begin and end up programming projects. In this structure every programmer's proficiency is needed from the point of creating an idea to implementing it. Scrum currently boasts high appeal just because of its simplicity, efficiency and broad applicability in terms of controlling diverse interactive and incremental tasks. This agile software development structure is generally associated with Ken Schwaber, the owner of a business called Advanced Advancement Approaches. He used something that would later be Scrum in 1990s.

Other huge names pointed out include John Scumniotales, Jeff McKenna and Jeff Sutherland. In 1995 and the following years Ken Schwaber and Jeff Sutherland combined to form the present Scrum methodology. An imperative system is called sprint and each consists of a list of activities that an advancement group feels it has enough time to work on. This list is called a sprint backlog. When developing the backlog, the programmers focus on how rapidly they performed their past sprints. They breakdown the stories and features into littler tasks that are set to be completed within four to 16 hours.

The list is developed in a way that permits each developer to choose a job in relation to the pre-set scope of work and their level of knowledge and abilities. This, as clarified above, promotes group cohesion and teamwork. The status of work that's pending, in development or completed is made a record of in the task board. Scrum involves major and auxiliary roles. The previous are called pigs while the latter are called chickens. Moreover, the major roles are normally the ones that cause the production of an item and they're 3. The first one is called the ScrumMaster. It oversees the nimble software development procedure to make sure that it is followed by the development team without disturbances. It gets rid of barriers and is not always a boss.

The Scrum Master just stands between the programming group and any possible interference. The second role is the Product Owner who ensures that the specialists' deliverables are according to the customer's expectations. Besides, the Product Owner puts jobs in the Sprint stockpile in the order of priority so that the Advancement Group can select the jobs they want to finish for each sprint. Last but not least there is the Development Group, generally a cross-functional group, which presumes the duty of doing a shows project. Its duty is to deliver a valuable item that is well worth shipping to a customer at the end of each sprint. A typical agile software application development group is made up of three to nine specialists that have varied skills. Their work is to examine, design and test a product. They also solve technical problems through a collective method

CHAPTER 1: WHAT IS SCRUM?

Scrum is an easy task management framework for incremental product development that has ended up being extremely well-known in the software development community. Normally paired with engineering practices from the eXtreme Programming (XP) community, Scrum is one exponent of the nimble movement and represents a paradigmatic shift from "waterfall," a traditional job management technique that, until recently, has controlled software application development.

The Scrum approach is deliberately developed as a framework-i.e., a lightweight management wrapper that can be applied to existing processes. Nevertheless, every part of Scrum's minimal structure is necessary for its core tenets of assisting in performance through communication, partnership, and self-organization. Given its spare structure, it is vital that all of Scrum's roles and processes are observed. Here's a quick overview of Scrum's primary roles and meetings.

Scrum Functioning
The Scrum structure consists of only 3 roles: The Product Owner, the Scrum team, and the ScrumMaster.

1. The Product Owner is the single individual accountable for the success of a project, which requires communicating product vision to group members and negotiating sprint goals with them. As such, this person constantly reprioritizes the Item Backlog to reflect those products which will yield the highest business value. Because the Product Owner is accountable for producing a return on investment, this role possesses the authority to accept or turn down each item increment at the sprint review meeting, which happens at the conclusion of each sprint.

2. The Scrum team is a cross-functional and self-organizing team of about seven members (plus or minus two) that is accountable for delivering a practical item increment each sprint. Throughout the Sprint Planning meeting, the group works out the work it will deal with each sprint with the Product Owner and then, during the sprint, identifies amongst its members how to finish that work.

3. The ScrumMaster assists in team efficiency and self-organization by removing obstacles that block development, advising all group members to observe Scrum's guidelines, and making sure that all Scrum artifacts remain highly visible. It is very important to keep in mind that the ScrumMaster has no authority. This role operates as a servant-leader. Therefore, it is advised that people who obtain fulfillment from a group's success, not just individual heroics, are best fit for this position.

Scrum Conferences
The Scrum framework consists of 4 primary meetings (Sprint Planning, the Daily Standup, Sprint Reviews, and the Sprint Retrospectives) and one important supplementary meeting Stockpile Grooming.

1. During the Sprint Planning meeting, the Product Owner and the group negotiate the work that team members will attempt to finish in the next sprint. The Product Owner is responsible

for identifying the work with the highest priority, while the team is accountable for committing to the amount of work it can accomplish within the confines of the sprint.

2. The Daily Standup meeting enables team members to deliver updates and exchange information every day. Every day, at the same time and place, group members spend fifteen minutes reporting to one another. Each staff member reports to the rest of the team what he or she did since the prior meeting, what will be done before the next one, and what obstacles block progress.

3. The Sprint Evaluation meeting happens at the end of each sprint. At this meeting, the group demonstrates the functioning product increment it has developed and the Product Owner either accepts or turns down the work, based upon the previously negotiated agreement. This is an opportunity to "examine and adjust"- that is, to examine the item's progress and revise direction, if needed, for future sprints.

4. The Sprint Retrospective offers the team with an occasion to inspect and adapt its own procedures. During this meeting, the group contemplates its performance in the past sprint and brainstorms ways to enhance going forward.

5. Backlog Grooming, which is known as the 5th Scrum meeting, creates a dedicated time for the Product Owner and group to come together to prepare the stockpile before the Sprint Planning meeting.

Although Scrum is a relatively skeletal framework, it is necessary that professionals acknowledge how purposeful its construction is. Each role of the framework is designed to develop a balance-in terms of both authority and responsibility-for the members of a Scrum team, while Scrum's few meetings and artifacts sketch out needed turning points within the development cycle. Naturally, there are ways in which organizations can modify the structure to suit specific needs, but these basic elements should stay intact and provide users with a roadmap for reliable, continuously improving item development and delivery

CHAPTER 2: SCRUM MASTERS

In the IT sphere, a lot of different principles and methods are applied during every phase of the software application development lifecycle. They help to make the development and screening procedures be more versatile and efficient.
Scrum is just one of such a nimble methodology. It speeds up the procedure of item development and software testing procedure. Scrum has several particular qualities.
What Are Scrum's Main Characteristics?
It integrates 2 techniques: complex and versatile.
The procedure includes 3 parties: Product Owner, scrum master and development and screening team.
The method needs a reliable communication and productive partnership between all stakeholders of the development procedure.
A scrum master is an irreplaceable member of the development procedure who offers an effective adoption of the agile software application development methodology. This person can be called the inter link between marketing and development departments.
An unavoidable part of daily life of the group members are the stand-up meetings. They take place every day with the aim of keeping the stakeholders informed about the status of the development and testing treatments.
What Are the Core Aspects of the Daily Meeting?
The scope of work what has already been done.
The work prepare for a day.
The trouble spots.
The conversation of these elements helps to recognize the real state of affairs and to define further actions and steps of the development process. The exchange of info might stop the incident of issues.
The communication needs to be effective on every phase of software development life process. For example, it is unrealistic to perform usability screening or functional testing of a high quality without sharing the gotten results and known truths. The exact same circumstance is with the development process.

The scrum master enables the team to work as a single entity. It is rather hard to be a really good scrum master. This person must have some particular qualities.
What Are the Attributes of a Great Scrum Master?
He has the ability to promote the efficient work of the group and each its member.
The scrum master is always ready to help or to give a piece of advice to resolve and prevent any troubles and problems.
This person knows with the majority of scrum rules and concepts. He shares these information with the members of his group The scrum master is a coach for the team.
The master is a wise time planner. He is able to figure out an approximate time needed for solving this or that issue.

He is the source of motivation for the team. The scrum master knows how to inspire the specialists and how to raise the team spirit.
The scrum master never over controls the group.

Why Scrum?
The word 'scrum' is derived from the game of rugby where a group collectively moves down the field to reach its objective. Scrum is an empirical procedure that encourages teams to challenge themselves a little bit more every time. Scrum follows a procedure of 'Inspect' and 'Adapt'. Regular examination exposes issues or barriers and the group then adapts its method as needed. This much shorter feedback loop makes sure that any product defects are repaired early in the cycle.
Scrum is made up of certain roles, artifacts and time boxes. A Scrum group is comprised of 5-7 people. Let us have a brief look at the different components of Scrum.
There is normally one Product Owner who functions as the consumer or customer proxy and settles the requirements. The Scrum Master is the procedure owner who primarily works on removing any barriers the team faces and ensures that Scrum is followed correctly. The Team is any employee besides the Product Owner or Scrum Master. This could be a developer, tester, business expert, architect and so on. Scrum encourages its group members to wear different hats and it is very typical to find group members pitching in as and where needed.
Scrum is comprised of iterations or 'sprints'. These might have any length varying from one week to 4 weeks. Sprints begin and end at a fixed time irrespective of whether the targeted work is finished. This element is called a 'time box' which will be explained right below in more detail.

Scrum Artifacts
The main artifacts that are produced in Scrum are the Item Stockpile, Sprint Backlog, Sprint Burndown and Release Burndown.
The Product Backlog is an ordered list of all the functions that the client may want in the product. The highest concern functions are at the leading making sure that the most crucial and highest value functionality is built first.

The Sprint Backlog has a restricted scope. It consists of functions from the Item Backlog that are going to be constructed in that specific sprint. Any work that is not done at the end of the sprint returns to the item stockpile for reprioritization.
The Sprint Burndown chart tells us how much time is left before we reach our goal. It tracks the work done every day and is relevant only for the given sprint.
The Release Burndown chart tracks the time left up to the end of the release. It also depicts how much work is finished with respect to launch goals.

Scrum Timeboxes
Scrum introduces the idea of a time box. This means that an offered event will have a fixed time and will end at the end of the time limitation. The numerous meetings in Scrum are allocated a timebox. The Scrum time boxes include the Sprint planning meeting, Release planning meeting, the Daily Scrum, Sprint review and retrospectives. The Daily Scrum or standup is always 15

minutes. The other planning conferences also have a fixed time depending upon the Sprint length that the group selects.

Scrum Acceptance Criteria

Scrum introduces the idea of 'done'. This is also called success criteria or approval requirements and lays out the conditions a particular feature need to meet in order to be considered 'done' or complete.

Scrum Story Boards and Junction

The story board - used to represent the Sprint Backlog - is another pillar of the Scrum procedure. This is a physical board in the team which could be part of a wall or some walls as needed. There is a principle of a 'story' which is a feature or high level requirement. Normally, any item from the product stockpile could turn into one or a lot of stories. The story mentions what the user accepts from an offered feature. For example, 'As a user, I should have the ability to visit to my e-mail'. The success criteria lay out the things that must happen to consider this 'done'. All the tasks needed to strategy, design, code and test this story are positioned under this. These tasks could be done by some people on the team.

Scrum motivates collocating all the group members in an open group area minus walls. The idea is to encourage open communication and decrease overheads from e-mails or call. Impromptu conversations between the consumer and group members are pretty common in a Scrum room.

Info Radiators

The Scrum artifacts are shown throughout the area where the team sits and works. These include story boards, backlogs, burndown charts, barrier section, architecture maps, designs etc. The idea is that any relevant information should be easily noticeable to the group all the time. This is useful and also motivational. The info radiates or jumps out from all the charts and boards. Color coding is used to distinguish tasks, stories, barriers and so on. A ton of software tools are available for tracking Scrum projects, but it cannot change the impact physical info radiators have in my opinion.

Sprint Retrospective

The retrospective deserves unique mention. This is where the team comes together at the end of a sprint and openly speaks about what worked out and what could be done better. A retrospective is not to be used for finger pointing. Retrospectives become more reliable as a team gels and group members trust one another and the management. This is needed to reveal impediments that people may be reluctant to speak about in a typical controlling management structure.

CHAPTER 3: SCRUM IN THE GLOBAL COMMUNITY

Although Scrum encourages collocation, it may not always be possible, specifically in the case of dispersed teams that are in several geographical places. Scrum has been proven to be efficient even in such situations and a lot of teams practice distributed Scrum.

This is a high level introduction to Scrum, we will be taking a closer and more comprehensive look at the various Scrum ideas talked about in this book.

How to Choose a Scrum Master

In their capability as scrum master, one's duty is to guide, oversee and facilitate that the scrum work process is unimpeded, and used efficiently to ensure higher efficiency in item development projects.

However, for scrum to be successful, it is extremely crucial that all those purchased it, be it the Scrum Master, Product Owner or Development Team, comprehend the nature of their duties and therefore do what is expected of them, which will not be possible until and unless, all these roles are well-understood by those designated to them.

Usually, when an unexpected switch is made from other agile techniques to scrum, there might be some difficulties in selecting the scrum master, for it is a crucial post that must be filled by exactly the right prospect.

The position might be designated either by the work team itself, or chosen by senior management that is not associated with the daily working of these projects. The question is, how should the choice about the appointment of the scrum master be made?

The answer depends on comprehending the nature of work that being a scrum master entails, and which sort of person appropriates for it. The person appointed for this job is usually connected with servant-leader qualities, which indicates that he maintains a balance between leading the group, and working for it to ensure that there are no obstacles in its working process.

While he is definitely a figure of authority, the master must recognize that the decision regarding the product development technique within scrum is that of the development team; he needs to only have an advisory role in that capacity. Bulk of his work is to plan and set up conferences, establish communication between the Product Owner and development group and safeguard the latter from dealing with interruptions of any kind. For that reason, the master needs to be an individual of experience that has superior managerial skills, and dilemma management capabilities.

It is usually presumed that the position of scrum master resembles that of a project manager, and therefore, if the former arrangement was such, he/she can be designated into this new office. Nevertheless, it is necessary to remember that a project manager works in a more reliable capacity where final approval for everything is in his hands. Since, the scenario is not rather as comparable in the case of the latter, typically a problem might emerge if the Project manager is unable to comprehend the nature of change that it imbues.

Some groups also follow a system where the master is continually rotated, possible with different projects or different Product Owners. Many people actually believe that this is not a really stereo, as constant change in management enables different result each time over. Such a system will be useful only when the group is wanting to create learning opportunities, and wants to educate all group members remaining in such a position, before choosing who shall be best for a long-lasting plan.

Stay with the Scrum Rules (Come What May).
The Scrum Guidelines exist as the standard basics of an outstanding framework. However, these rules are continuously tested when we try to apply them in market. What makes it so essential to adhere to these guidelines?
The next tip is based on an example from market that really tested my experience and rely on the scrum structure. I wrote it because in my experience, the single most difficult thing within market, is having the willpower and faith to stay with the scrum guidelines.
This pointer is extremely closely associated to starting with the scrum guidelines, but discreetly different. Whereas that rule was all about beginning on the right foundation, this rule is all about sticking to that structure throughout thick and thin. It may appear as if basic guidelines are easy to stick to, but any knowledgeable scrum practitioner will tell you that 'simple to comprehend' does not always equal 'easy to implement'.
Let us take the example of the everyday scrum. I remember a situation in which, as a result of certain aspects, sprint planning took more than the suggested four hours for a two-week sprint. In keeping with scrum rules we time-boxed the meeting and decided to reunite the next day to finish the session. Because the 2nd meeting was in the early morning, the group questioned the need for an everyday scrum meeting, especially since each of us knew what the other was doing the day before (planning) and what we would do (planning). They actually ended up being quite psychological and practically defiant about the situation. As a scrum master, I had to remind them that the everyday scrum was also a source of communication about issues. Live concerns, blockers for planning, concerns that had been communicated by e-mail to certain members, absolutely anything. Thus, this fifteen-minute stand-up meeting was most likely more important after 4 hours of planning, since communication might have been missed since we had not discussed anything but preparing for the former day. If we had broken the basic rule of having a daily scrum every day, we may have missed the chance to solve and communicate about an issue that would have postponed our sprint or release.

This is just a small example of how sticking to a very fundamental rule can have a very big impact on the efficiency of a group and I am certain that if you look through the scrum guidelines you can think of a lot of other ramifications of losing out scrum rules. For that reason I would advise you to stick to the scrum guidelines and learn how to give reasonable descriptions of why each scrum rule is so important.

CHAPTER 4: LESSENING RISKS THROUGH SCRUM

Being an Agile, iterative procedure, the Scrum framework inherently minimizes risk. The following Scrum practices assist in the reliable management of risk:

1. Flexibility minimizes business-environment-related risk.

Risk is mainly decreased in Scrum because of the flexibility in including or customizing requirements at any time in the job lifecycle. This allows the organization to react to threats or chances from the business environment and unexpected requirements anytime they emerge, with normally low expense of managing such dangers.

2. Regular feedback minimizes expectations-related risk.

Being iterative, the Scrum framework gives sufficient chances to acquire feedback and set expectations throughout the project lifecycle. This guarantees that the job stakeholders, as well as the team, are not caught off guard by miscommunicated requirements.

3. Team ownership decreases estimation risk.

The Scrum Group approximates and takes ownership of the Sprint Backlog Products, which causes more precise estimation and prompt delivery of product increments.

4. Openness minimizes non-detection risk.

The Scrum principle of transparency around which the structure is built makes sure that dangers are discovered and communicated early, leading to better risk handling and mitigation. Furthermore, when carrying out Scrum of Scrums Meetings, Impediments that one group is currently dealing with might be deemed a danger for other Scrum Teams in the future. This should be acknowledged in the Updated Impediments Log.

5. Iterative delivery decreases financial investment risk.

Continuous delivery of value throughout the Scrum project lifecycle, as possibly shippable Deliverables are created after every Sprint, lowers financial investment risk for the client.

Let me clarify by giving few reasons for Why Scrum Always Works:

1) Communication shouldn't be the barrier.

Communication amongst the members of the team and the clients is what gets appreciated and promoted by Scrum, which leads to attitude helpful for the group.

2) Amazingly Fast Results.

Getting the results after every few steps is what needed to get the feedback from the client, which works so good and practical to work effectively in the job.

3) Stay focused.

Time waste is just not the focus in this method as every little thing gets prioritised based on the importance of the item.

4) Estimates the reasonable time.
Production team's involvement makes it much easier and fair to estimate the precise time needed.

5) Arranged on own.
One of the jobs of the production group is to make sure to achieve the defined objective on preferred time. A mix of capability and ability levels are often best to promote a continuous work flow.

6) Open.
Scrum is always transparent: From the start, the customer knows on what he could expect at the end of each step as he is the hand behind the item stockpile. Within the team also they maintain equal openness, in simple fact they primary it throughout the job.

CHAPTER 5: SCRUM AND PITFALLS TO PREVENT INDEFINITELY

Scrum, having its roots in Agile method, can be successfully employed for practically any type of project. However, scrum is most chosen for software development purposes. The scrum process is ideally suited for rapidly changing task environments. It is most useful, and its potential can be tapped in the best way, when the user associated requirements are changed frequently, or arbitrarily, because of various reasons. The approach makes it possible to include the changes easily and efficiently within its development cycle, and still create positive outputs.

The true essence and working of scrum.
According to scrum methodology, development takes place in other words bursts of activity called "sprints". Each sprint can generally last from two to 4 weeks. Each sprint begins with a meeting, referred to as a "sprint meeting", and usually concludes with clearly defined and set out development goals. Sprint conferences are really short, and happen daily before the commencement of the sprint for that particular day. The primary objective of the meeting is to apprise everyone about how much development progress has been made since the prior day, and what objectives are to be attained on the specific working day. The main purpose of scrum is to help the team members in inspecting and adapting to the changes, and supplying transparency with regards the working of the project. Another primary benefit offered by scrum framework is to increase the involvement, and the interaction of the customer with the team members. The customer remains apprised about the most current development status, which helps him or her to carry out educated choices about what further development activities are required to finish the task in totality, and what features and performances need to be left out, or which have become redundant throughout the development cycle.

Traps while carrying out scrum.
Scrum is a framework, an approach based upon an arranged thought procedure developed specifically to accommodate changing development requirements, and the main issue with Agile and scrum is that the methodology is to be carried out, or its rules enforced in a correct way. Many a times, when companies are not appropriately trained in the execution of the method, there is a tendency to fall back upon old development methods, purposely or unconsciously, hence making scrum redundant. Conventional development techniques such as Waterfall have been in existence since a long period of time, and people are more acquainted with them. Task managers have practiced these approaches for a very long time, and they are more proficient with them. Scrum can be hard to execute, and if the supervisor is not properly trained, she or he may substitute some of the scrum associated procedures with Waterfall methods. The goal is to offer a particular solution throughout the development cycle, and when the person fails to implement scrum in a specific development related procedure, he or she "spots" up scrum execution procedure with a Waterfall technique. This should be kept away from at all expenses. Scrum must be implemented in totality for it to be efficient.

5 reasons THE SCRUM MASTER FUNCTION works

Reasons

1. Committed bulldozer: Unlike other frameworks, the role focuses someone on getting rid of barriers. This means that the team can focus on finishing the job.

2. Committed coach: The role gives one-person obligation for coaching others. Nobody can "pass the dollar" on this. Thus, a single person has the focus of helping all members of the organisation to understand the framework.

3. Impartiality: A scrum master can be as practical to a group as a product owner (see below) without selecting sides. The only focus is on making certain the structure and job succeeds. This can help resolve issues and acquire trust.

4. Obligation for structure not delivery: This is practically reverse psychology. The scrum master is only interested in making sure the framework is carried out as the scrum guidelines say. Separating the obligation for the framework from the responsibility to provide means that she or he can focus on making sure that rules are followed which in turn develops a well-oiled device. If the scrum master's job is done and everybody in the scrum team is performing their role, then the development group can deliver.

5. No single point of control that could flop: Since a scrum master doesn't control the team, the absence of one does not leave the team in disarray. The scrum master sets up a system that everyone can follow in his or her lack.

5 reasons why THE Product Owner ROLE works
The Reasons
1. Time maximised for business return on investment: The Product Owner is not accountable for delivering the work or maintaining the procedure but just for making top priority calls and keeping the requirements backlog. This permits a great deal of focus.

2. Dedicated source of requirements: There is no one else in the organisation that needs to be sought advice from on a project's requirements. Senior stakeholder requirements flow through the Product Owner for a single point of contact.

3. One person accountable for changes in requirements: As the business picture changes only one person needs to capture the new requirements and update them.

4. Accomplishes the best compromise: Even senior stakeholders will really need to trust their Product Owner with the decision. This aligns the business and makes appropriate compromises for the good of the item.

5. Aligns the consumer and team, day-to-day: This role is the interface between the business and the team. Her/his presence at all the scrum meetings means that the group is always acting upon the most recent info.

5 reasons THE DEVELOPMENT TEAM ROLE works

Reasons

1. A group of devoted experts: Clearly calling the group out as experts, means that scrum groups are assembled to resolve issues on their own. This maximizes other roles to focus on their own areas of know-how.

2. Versatile to business needs: Scrum teams adapt to an offered situation so as to get a product increment built. Any decisions should be connected only to a company requirement. This in turn gives a company long and short-term flexibility and lowers squandered effort in favour of targeted effort.

3. Lean and cost effective: The little size integrated with high degree of expertise means that things get done to a high degree of quality with minimal technical communication.

4. Less management needed: Teams arrange themselves. This means that everyone else can focus on his/her own role.

5. Highly scalable when given the resource: Big groups can be split up and arranged through routine meetings called scrum-of-scrums. The teams each have scrum masters to keep them coordinated. Caution - when 2 or more groups work on the exact same code-base, the team will need to decide if this is practical.

CHAPTER 6: UNDERSTANDING A SCRUM MASTER, A PRODUCT OWNER, AND DEVELOPMENT TEAM

The success of Scrum is nearly completely dependent on the various members of the Scrum structure, and their understanding and emulation of the particular responsibilities in whatever classification they're inhabiting.

Nevertheless, in some instances, especially when a sudden switch is made to this agile method, people might not fully understand the nature of their duties in the work procedure. Let us consider exactly what the role of the scrum master, Product Owner and development team is, respectively.

The Scrum Master is the servant-leader in scrum. This indicates that his leadership is limited within the purview of guaranteeing that the Development team doesn't face any obstacles in the course of their work. He also establishes the channel of communication between the Product Owner and the group, alongside being accountable for dilemma management, if and when the need emerges. The Scrum Master schedules the conferences and makes sure that the working group is able to perform efficiently by determining and getting rid of all sources of obstacle and diversion.

The Product Owner, on the other hand, is in some ways the representative of the customer. The standard role here is to guarantee that the business output produced meets the requirements of the customer. For this to be accomplished, the Product Owner writes customer centric items, organizes them in order of concern and then adds them to the product stockpile for the development team to work upon. The lattermost of these - writing the item backlog - is among the most important of all Scrum procedures, and should thus be done with utmost intelligence and care to detail. Hence, the Product Owner should be someone of great skill and experience in that regard.

Product Owner is the single individual who is accountable for the success of the task. The Scrum Product Owner communicates his/her vision to the software application development group, outlines work to be finished in the stockpile, and prioritizes it based on business value. Obviously, she or he should also work carefully with stakeholders (to guarantee their interests are reflected in the product) and the software application development team (to ensure the product is developed on time and within spending plan). As such, the Scrum Product Owner should be readily available to the development team to offer direction and answer questions.

However, this mix of authority and accessibility to the team makes it hard for the Product Owner to resist the temptation to micro-manage. As the Scrum method of agile software development values self-organization, it is the Product Owner's responsibility to appreciate the team's capability to complete its work based upon its own plan. This means that a Product Owner can't add work mid-sprint. Even if requirements change or a chief competitor takes an item to market that renders plans unimportant, the Product Owner should wait until the next sprint planning meeting to reroute a team's trajectory. (You can imagine how difficult it is to maintain a hands-off technique to management when deadlines approach and consumers make last-minute needs).

Moreover, the Scrum Product Owner is accountable for constantly considering what activities will yield the greatest business value. This means making difficult - even out of favor - decisions during the sprint planning meeting. But, again, as the Product Owner is the single individual who takes the heat if the job fails, he or she must strongly stake out what elements of an item are important, when they are built, and so on. Just as the team has an obligation to deliver the negotiated work to the Product Owner, the Product Owner is obliged to deliver the item to the customer, according to the consumer's requirements.

Using Scrum to manage agile software application development is the leading method to help teams lower risk and associated expenses, while increasing the quality of a group's releases. Through an emphasis on communication and cooperation, Scrum brings everybody together-- from designers to stakeholders-- to build a much better product.

The group members have cross-functional skills and plan, design, develop, test, examine and so on, all themselves, with each employee bringing their own expertise to the leading edge.

Such a group should be experienced in creating and sustaining a harmonious work relationship and group characteristics so as to ensure that their consistent interaction was actually without any problems.

The bottom line here is that the integrated working of the 3 entities - the Scrum Master, the Product Owner and Development Group - is what makes scrum a nimble method producing superior results. Nevertheless, appointment to these positions must be made really thoroughly in order to ensure that each person's strengths are recognized.

The scrum master in some organizations is continually turned. Such radical steps, however, should be considered only if it the company is aiming to create learning chances and recognize everyone's abilities and weaknesses. If Scrum is being implemented as it must be, with time boxed sprints being carried out, and product and sprint stockpiles being preserved well, this nimble method can lead to a noticeable boost in a firm's performance.

CHAPTER 7: SOME COMMON PROBLEMS THAT A SCRUM MASTER FACES

The Scrum Master has the primary role of facilitating this work technique and making sure that there is no obstacle in the team's efforts at achieving their sprint target. However, small glitches and unforeseen mistakes always occur, and some are so common that all scrum masters should have some prepared or potential solutions all set for them. It is not only time-saving and efficient, but also enables the sharpening of one's crisis management abilities in the long run.

One of the most common problems that occur is that the Product Owner is not able to give the group the product backlog in time. Not knowing the concerns of the Product Owner, it is challenging for a development group to go forth in action.

In such a scenario, the scrum master can choose from among different alternatives, depending upon the exact circumstances. Either the entire team could be enabled to take a break from sprinting, specifically if the hold-up is supposed to be by a day or two. On the other hand, a development group could also carry on with its planning meetings without giving top priority to backlog, especially if the team has already completed some effective sprints.

The group can then develop a rough draft of concerns if they recognize with the general direction the product is taking and present it to the Product Owner for approval or change. Aside from that, the team could take this break as a chance to examine their work and gather feedback so as to further enhance the scrum process.

Nevertheless, to ensure that the scrum pattern is followed, a stringent policy should be followed wherein such breach of process is unacceptable. If extreme circumstances are faced, the sprint completion can work upon a model of incentives too. Apart from this, in most circumstances, overseas units are usually uninformed of Scrum and how it works. For that reason, correct training, albeit a concise, brief one need to be carried out for otherwise the cruising shall not be smooth.

Many scrum masters also face the question of whether it shall be better for a whole development team work on a specific aspect, finish the corresponding sprint and move on to the next, or the group be divided with numerous different groups handing different aspects at the exact same time.

The solution to this dilemma depends on different factors such as size of the group, the time restrictions, the nature of the task, and so on etc. Typically a master might choose to try both the techniques before picking one as the standard, or choose not to have a basic technique at all.

A knowledgeable scrum master typically does has some such options at hand to deal with such limitations. However, being prepared ahead of time is always best, for it shows insight and efficiency that are both incredibly important for business matters.

WHAT MAKES A FANTASTIC PRODUCT OWNER?

Here are a few qualities that I feel are essential to be a reliable Product Owner:
Overall Dedication - complete engagement with the Scrum team is essential. While it may not be possible to be physically present in a Scrum team room all the time, the PO needs to be

readily available by means of email, social media, messenger etc. The idea is to appear approachable so that the team members do not wait to voice their questions.

Product Backlog owner - the PO owns the Item Backlog. This is a purchased list of all the features that are desirable in the item. The PO constantly orders this according to changing business concerns and must be on hand to answer any questions concerning the backlog.

Subject Matter Professional - As a specialist who needs to know the business and the product completely, the PO is the go-to person for the Scrum group to answer any product related questions. He is the sole authority on the product and should be able to explain any business reasoning or in-depth performance that needs to be built in, and thus should assist the team as they work on their Sprint jobs.

Collaborative - Being collaborative and a great communicator is essential for the PO. He ought to have the ability to position himself 'at par' with the Scrum group and be open to deal with them at a peer level. A modification in frame of mind may be needed here! Although the person who is the PO is much higher in the organizational hierarchy, he/she needs to mix into the team and work shoulder to carry to achieve the common objective.

Scrum Vs Extreme Programming
Agile Process.
The Agile Process or software development refers to a set of software application development approaches which are based on iterative development. In this process, the options and requirements both develop mutual collaboration between cross functional teams. These teams are self-organizing in nature.

The Agile software application development approach usually promotes a regimented sort of project management process which encourages:
1. Regular adjustment and examination.
2. Self-organization and responsibility.
3. A leadership approach which promotes teamwork.
4. A firm method which bring into line the development with client needs and company objectives.
5. And a group of best engineering practices having an objective to enable quick delivery of good-quality software application.

Extreme Programming (EP)
It is a software development approach with an objective to boost software application responsiveness and quality to the volatile requirements of customers. Being a kind of Agile procedure, it promotes regular releases in little development cycles. This introduces checkpoints and enhances the productivity in a way that the new requirements from consumers can be adopted.

The advantages of Extreme Programming are:
1. Unit testing of all code.
2. Avoiding programming of functions till needed.
3. Programming in sets or performing extensive code evaluation.

4. Clarity and simplicity in code.
5. Volatile customer requirements better understood.
6. A flag management structure.
7. Regular communication between the programmers and even with the consumer.

The disadvantages of Extreme programming are:
1. No documented compromises of user conflicts.
2. Unstable requirements.
3. Absence of general design document or requirements.
4. Integrates insufficient software design.
5. Requires conferences at reoccurring intervals at substantial expenditure to clients.
6. Can increase the size of the risk of scope creep because of the lack of comprehensive requirements documents.
7. Requires excess of cultural change to adopt.

Differences between Scrum and Extreme Programming(EP):
1. The time period for iterative sprints is different in both techniques.
2. Modifications are not allowed by the Scrum groups during their sprints. Whereas Extreme Programming groups need to be much more agreeable to changes.
3. Work is done by EP groups in rigorous priority order. Whereas in case of Scrum, the Product Owner focuses on the set of activities.
4. EP does prescribe some engineering practices; Scrum doesn't.

CHAPTER 8: SCRUM-AGILE PROJECT MANAGEMENT SOFTWARE

Using Scrum job management software application is an easy way of understanding big quantities of data and putting it into different forms that are easier to comprehend, such as graphs or charts. Big projects, with lots of information, can be challenging without the appropriate software.

Noted below are some features of scrum and nimble software application and how they can aide you in running your business. You will also be notified of the ways in which this software can help you in organizing information.

Owning the Information: When there is a lot of info to be taken into an orderly form, it can at times take control of your life and make running a company even more challenging. Scrum will help you control the info, not the other way around.

Refining Your Info: Scrum project management software application helps you to organize and gather your info. Agile job management software will fine-tune that organized information and turn it into something that is more versatile and workable.

Nimble software is run and organized by people, rather than by computer systems alone. This allows your data to be optimised with human intelligence and created to be comprehended by routine people, not necessarily just computer systems.

Group Building: Scrum needs groups to communicate and always be on top of the job which they are handling. This software has features, like backlogging and sprinting, which enable records to be more easily stored.

While team work is a major requirement, self-organization is a thing which is greatly promoted by scrum software. While it helps you to organize the information, it must be updated and made a record of correctly so it functions as it should. This is where the group enters play.

Keeping Logs: Along with tape-recording information, logs-- like time boxes, product schedule and production and profits salary-- can be saved also. In simple fact many businesses find scrum software to be rather useful when it concerns logging stats like these. Agile task management software boosts this ability by offering methodology that produces smoother information entry, storage, and organization. Obtaining and preserving customer feedback is also simpler to track. Keeping up with ever-changing trends in the market and within the consumer world can be tough. With this software, business management and team communication can be simplified. Nimble software and scrum project management software application go together when it pertains to organizing, maintaining, and adapting info.

SCRUM APPROVAL CRITERIA

Prior To a Product Owner would ever deem a group's work "done" she or he would always consult the corresponding user story's approval criteria. In the Scrum technique of nimble software application development, acceptance requirements are the requirements which should be met for a story to be finished. Acceptance criteria are vital to Scrum's management success since they clearly communicate a Product Owner's expectations and a team's development objectives in one fell swoop. There is no gray area. Any member of the team, at any time, can speak with a story's acceptance requirements and be assured that, if the requirements listed are satisfied by the end of the sprint, the team will receive credit for its work.

But what happens when only some-or even the majority-of a story's acceptance criteria is met? Does the group receive a matching percentage of the story points for the fraction of work they completed? The easy answer is no. Scrum prevents Product Owners from granting partial credit to work that is, fittingly, only partially completed. All of the requirements need to be met or the work is declined as incomplete. In truth, many ScrumMasters will not enable teams to present work that has not been finished.

Why does Scrum promote this all-or-nothing view of development? There are some reasons for this. To start with, an implicit acceptance criterion of any story is that it ought to be completed within the sprint. Because work is restricted to the limits of a sprint, a team must appreciate that deadline for its work to be considered satisfactory. Second of all, groups commonly find that the final one percent of work to be finished - the final push of the sprint - is disproportionately labor-intensive and lengthy. Put another way, till it's done, it is not done.

Finally, awarding credit for incomplete work leads to velocity inflation. When a team's Product Owner awards credit for incomplete work, the group's speed is no longer a reliable metric and therefore has no value for forecasting. Additionally, when a team gets credit for a story that it actually has to finish in the next sprint, it means the next sprint consists of additional work that isn't represented in the sprint stockpile. Hence a group must work harder to compensate. Unsurprisingly, this practice usually causes a team falling farther and further behind, generating substantial technical financial obligation along the way.

Clearly, it is useful for both the Product Owner and the group to only award credit when it is completely made. Philosophically, it reinforces Scrum's tenets of openness and open communication and, practically, it makes it possible for accurate forecasting and prevents technical financial obligation.

CHAPTER 9: SIX ACTIONS TO A SCRUM CHANGE

Transitioning to scrum is no easy task, no matter the size of the organization. The bigger the company the harder it will be. I have seen far a lot of businesses spending exorbitant quantities in transforming to agile, yet fail in its attempts. I found that it is the direction or lack of that plays a major aspect. Here are 3 steps you need to require to get you begun in the right direction.

Step 1:
I have found the best way to shift is to begin with a goal and grasp of why you are moving in this direction. Transitioning to agile is trendy, but not a great reason to take your organization through it. So what is your reason? Do you want to line up business and IT? Or do you want to increase your speed to market? Do you want to increase group performance? Understand why and communicate it.

Step 2:
Outline your goals. Do your goals agree with the reason you choose to shift? If they do not, go back and review. Developing the goals will help you focus.

Step 3:
Consider the type of transition. Is this an enterprise change to Agile or a department one? If it is a department approach, ensure you reach out to all the departments that your group will connect to get their work done. Make a contract with these other line managers upfront that will cover approvals that might be required, change in procedure that may really need to be made. Remember the objective is to remove as many barriers early on out of the teams way as possible.

Step 4:
Comprehend your organizations corporate culture. Be get ready for the obstacles ahead. Is there something you can do to help change the civilization to be more conducive to Nimble thinking? If not, intend on how your group will be protected. Bear in mind Scrum is really all about self organized groups. These teams resolve issues and make decisions on the spot. If your corporate civilization is not in positioning with this and other scrum values, your group will be hitting brick in no time.

Step 5:
Choose the right project! Never ever start with a project that is a high risk task. This would be devastating. Start with a project that is low risk and mid-sized. There is definitely enough complexity to the shift, you do not really need to add to it by choosing the wrong job.

Step 6:
Using the objectives from step 2 produce an assessment. Baseline where you are today. This will help you monitor and drive the development of the shift.

SCRUM: SPRINT PLANNING: CAPACITY DRIVEN VERSUS VELOCITY DRIVEN PLANNING

The development group are the only ones that commit to providing a sprint. There are 2 common methods used to reach a dedication. Both of them are guides that a group can use to figure out how much work to take on.

Capacity Driven
Capacity driven planning means that the group commit on what they can deliver in a sprint, based upon proof of the number of hours worth of jobs they think they can finish. They observe a buffer to represent conferences and downtime. They then total the number of hours of sub-tasks in the sprint stockpile and only commit to stories till their capability is reached. This is valuable for groups that do not yet have a velocity and I have seen it work for the period of a project to great influence.

The main thing is in adjusting the buffer based on retrospective. For instance:
- In a two-week sprint there are nine 7.5 hour days (not including planning day if meetings take all day). This is: 67.5 hours
- If we observe a buffer of 1.5 hours daily (13.5 hours) to represent lunch and conferences. This works out 67.5 - 13.5 = 54 hours a sprint for work.
- Thus the group commit to no greater than 54 hours of work in a sprint.
The buffer can be expanded or contracted each sprint, and you will quickly reach a foreseeable number of hours that are lost to scheduled conferences and other immoveable impediments. This is of course not fool-proof, but it is really close in my opinion.

Velocity Driven
Speed driven planning means that the team commit on how many stories they can deliver in a sprint based upon empirical proof of the amount of story points they provided per sprint till that point. The number of story points per sprint is called the average speed. For example:

- The team's average speed is 50 points per sprint
- They talk about and think that they were overly enthusiastic before and hurried the job, thus they minimize partially to 45 points (since they hardly delivered the final five point story in their last sprint).
The first 3 to 4 sprints are generally needed to set a trusted speed, for that reason if it is their first sprint, they use their gut feeling as a team to choose stories.

Which one is best?
Both capability driven and velocity driven techniques can work, but I have found that velocity driven planning tends to count on gut feeling more for the first few sprints till the team are in full swing. Capacity driven planning can incorrectly make teams think that the hours estimates are expected to be accurate (which they're not). I would suggest that capability driven planning yields better results for new teams who have not run a sprint together previously, since the empirical proof of job estimate is stronger and generally based upon something everybody in the group has done. I say this since speed driven planning is based on story points, whose relationship to time is less predictable in the early sprints.

CHAPTER 10: SCRUM EFFORT ESTIMATES AND STORY POINTS

What is the best way for task supervisors to budget and allocate the time team members have to invest in a project? Depending upon how the job will be managed-using conventional practices or nimble management techniques, for example-determine whether capability should be considered in terms of hours (time) or approximated difficulty (effort).

In traditional job management, supervisors approximate an employee's capacity for work based on task level planning. That is, they approximate just how long they expect particular tasks will take to be finished and after that designate jobs based upon a team member's total available time using traditional tools like Gantt charts. The problem with this technique is that it may lend itself to managing at the team member level, not the task level. That is, the Project manager might wind up focusing too much on keeping people busy and micromanaging individual work, instead of the overall success of the job being developed and the value it creates for the consumer. In complex new project development, like software teams, effort evaluation utilizing story points may be a much better answer than managing jobs.

Scrum, a well-known task management structure developed by nimble experts Ken Schwaber and Jeff Sutherland, takes a dramatically different perspective for determining how to track and report on project status. Rather than trying to keep group members busy, it concentrates on shippable item increment each sprint or work cadence. (That is, it ultimately puts the concentrate on the client, preferring to know that the consumer gets what it asked for, rather than keeping team members busy.) Groups can measure their general progress against this product increment making use of a focus on story-based estimate points.

How does this process of evaluation work? In a conference throughout which the boss/project manager is absent, teams approximate in abstracted figures to measure the relative effort associated with a particular story (a story is often made up of several tasks). Some teams use numeric sizing (i.e. a scale of 1 to 10) to estimate the "size" of a story, while others use tee shirt sizes (XS, S, M, L, XL, XXL, XXXL). Some use the Fibonacci sequence (1, 2, 3, 5, 8, 13, 21, 34, etcetera) to catch how trouble tends to increase significantly. Other groups have used dog types for evaluation purposes, in which, say, a teacup poodle or Chihuahua would represent the tiniest stories and a Fantastic Dane or Bull Mastiff would represent the biggest. What is necessary for effort estimation is that the group shares an comprehension of the scale it is using, so that everybody feels comfortable with the values of the scale.

Although the Project manager (or Product Owner, in Scrum) needs these estimates to successfully focus on backlog products and, subsequently, anticipate the delivery of the item to be developed based upon velocity, only the team can make these estimates and the presence of the task manager/Product Owner could pressure (purposefully or otherwise) a team to lessen its effort estimates. Even when group members estimate among themselves, it is recommended that everybody reveal their price quote at the exact same time to keep away from affecting others. This process looks like a game of poker in that individuals "show their hands"- or expose their estimates-simultaneously.

It just got better, didn't it? A big task and a cool new approach! Not rather, as is usually exposed on so many projects. Admittedly, the dialogue of the Project manager was simplified, but basically, this is how a great method is set up for failure.

Team member 1: 'Why do we really need to stand around? There are chairs around. We can just sit, right?'
Project manager: 'That is what the approach says."

TM 1: 'But why?'
Project manager: 'Something to do about if people stand, meetings are shorter'
TM2: 'But our meetings typically last for an hour or so and it is so tiring.'
Project manager: 'We have to go over so many concerns. Certainly it will take some time. If it is such a big offer, then you can sit.'
Therefore starts a slow, but consistent twisting of the tenets of Scrum and the group starts a slippery slope. As the team now begins to sit during 'Daily Stand Ups', the conferences increase in length from 1 hour to 1.5 hours, and sometimes stretching to 2 hours. With less time readily available for actual work, tensions increase. Team members start questioning the need to meet every day when on earlier projects they met once a week and things were more or less fine. Then from 'Daily Stand', the format changes to 'Alternate Day Sit Downs'. This impacts coordination and as the gap increases between conferences, the meetings begin taking a bit longer, or concerns increase.
Slowly, other changes start occurring - the whiteboard where tasks were updated in the first week stop being used by team members. Instead, they revert to sending e-mail updates. The Project manager, not recognizing the important significance of each of these tenets of Scrum, not trained in Scrum approaches and never having actually practiced Scrum, also starts questioning himself and accepts these changes. He keeps a track of 'To be done, In Process and Completed', but only at his desk. Other team members begin to become more confused.

Now as the group had dedicated itself to Scrum in the start, changing to alternate standard task management techniques in the middle of the project leads to an even larger mess. Outcome - a badly managed task which started off with good intentions of using Scrum as a methodology, but failed because of lack of comprehension of Scrum.

Scrum is an easy methodology but needs training in Scrum and assistance for first time users. Without it, important components wind up getting twisted and the job heads towards failure.

Moral of the story - Scrum training is not optional. If you want to get the best out of it, get professional assistance in the start and only after thorough training, should you use it at work. The SCRUM study is the global accreditation body for Scrum and Agile certifications. The quality of its study resources, use of technology to create easy to use procedures, streamlined partner registration and trainer accreditation procedure, and the concentrate on interactive training methodologies distinguishes it in the world of Scrum and Agile accreditations.
The scrum development method is based upon operating in sprints, which are brief time periods in which the team is able to produce incremental project deliverables. The Scrum

methodology makes use of three main roles, the ScrumMaster, who helps with the group, the Product Owner, who represents the business system that will use the software application and the Team, comprised of software application developers. Before each sprint, there is a preparation meeting with the entire group associated with the project to evaluate what was accomplished in the prior sprint and what will be accomplished in the next. Each sprint has a particular timeframe and if all the work is not finished, it enters into the "backlog" where the group can pull requirements for future sprints. The team has brief day-to-day conferences called "stand-ups" to discuss the task and how everyone is advancing and determine any obstacles to progress.

The scrum approach has lots of advantages, including versatility. The Product Owner doesn't really need to know all the requirements in the start of development and any new technology developed can be included into the new product. If one element of the product is not working or is not what the Product Owner wanted, it can be easily changed before anything is permanent. The Product Owner is involved in the entire development procedure so she or he can constantly provide feedback and reduce the risk of winding up with a product that is not useable. Moreover, as the group meets daily, anything that's not working is discovered rapidly.

The Scrum development approach can work well with an outsourced group even though it depends upon routine meetings. In order for the approach to work however, the team must meet every day. When 2 groups are working in different countries, daily "scrums" (stand-ups) enable them to stay on-task and engaged with the work of the off-site team members. So many groups make the off-site team appear closer through the application of video. The conferences go more smoothly when the group is operating in the same or similar time zones. Nearshoring, or contracting out to a country near to the company's county of origin, is ideal since it cuts down on language barriers and cultural distinctions, enabling the team to work well together. The similar time zone is also a key element for success. If the off-site group is working at the exact same time as the base team, they can join stand-ups and advertisement hoc meetings and ask questions throughout the day.

In standard software development approaches, the product requirements are given to the outsourced team at the start of the project; the overseas group produces an item and shows a completed product at the end. There is an absence of communication between Product Owner, the development company and the outsourced team. There could be tons of misunderstandings between the groups. The Scrum approach cuts down on those misconceptions between groups in different countries.

CHAPTER 11: WHAT IS VIRTUAL SCRUM AND HOW IS IT APPLIED?

Virtual scrum is an education tool used to help teach the scrum methodology to undergraduate students in the field of software application engineering. Since this has ended up being such a commonly used nimble practice in the software industry, it is necessary that students get a feel for this experience in a hands-on manner.

This research study provided an academic and hands-on technique to scrum methodology. This virtual training tool allowed students to familiarize themselves with programs and components of scrum like blackboards, web internet browsers, document viewers, charts and calendars.

Agile Software Development and the Scrum Methodology

Yearly studies have found that agile methods like scrum have been increasing every year. The 2007 State of Agile Advancement Study found that 37 percent of respondents use scrum. And today more than 50 percent of surveyed businesses have adopted scrum as their main agile method. This methodology is a trustworthy, shared approach to software development that can be implemented in any office. This also leverages communication and team work to effectively manage product development.

So while this study has established the value of virtual scrum, it is essential to comprehend how virtual scrum can be applied in your individual or workplace life. This research study was established to help users comprehend the framework and capabilities involved in the scrum methodology. Virtual scrum enables users to get a 3D experience inside the world of scrum development. This program helps users be involved in the scrum process by taking members through an incremental life process or sprints. These users are also able to be avatars with specific roles consisting of: Product Owner, Scrum Master and Scrum team.

It is essential to acquaint oneself with the fundamentals of this method before experiencing the virtual scrum world. This secondary tool, used to help people understand the procedure and actions involved throughout the scrum method, helps illustrate first-hand the advantages of this method. While reading and writing about the scrum approach is a great way to learn, it's specifically handy to get real direct exposure to the scrum procedure.

Virtual scrum not only permits users to take on important roles inside the scrum procedure, but it also helps people experience other aspects of scrum development consisting of organizing and creating user stories, planning the sprint backlog, keeping track of sprint work and completing the sprint. All of these essential steps to the procedure can be comprehended through virtual scrum. This teaching tool is incredibly important to the software application engineering world and many great companies are looking for engineers well-versed in this area. For those wanting to get a better grasp of scrum and its processes, using the virtual scrum program is an outstanding option. The simulated scrum environment may be the next significant trend in scrum education.